Welcome to a whole new world of lace!

"Delta" is the fourth letter of the Greek alphabet. The uppercase form of this letter is Δ. Since the mouth of a river sometimes has a triangular shape, it is often called a "river delta." For crocheters, "delta crochet" refers to crocheted fabric that is made using openwork triangles.

In Europe, where the technique originated, delta crochet was primarily used for thread work. When using thread, the fine-mesh created by this technique can be used in everything from doilies to fine-mesh clothing. By applying the same principles in projects using a heavier crochet cotton or yarn, you can create gorgeous apparel items and accessories that flatter everyone.

Delta crochet uses triangles. The "triangles" are formed using the taller crochet stitches—double crochet, treble crochet and double treble crochet. The fabric is created using these triangles with a string of chain stitches in between. The taller the stitch, the larger the mesh openings are!

Delta crochet can be worked side to side or in the round. One exciting feature of this technique is that the chains at the beginning of each row or round are very well hidden in the structure of the fabric. There are no unsightly seams or edges, and even unfinished edges have a very clean look.

This book includes instructions to make three mesh types—double crochet, treble crochet and double treble crochet. Once you have mastered making the mesh, there are five patterns to jump-start your creativity.

Try the technique with fashion yarns, bulky yarns and even thick-to-thin yarns. You will find that delta crochet will adapt to any thread or yarn out there, and I truly believe you will be surprised by how simple, yet beautiful, this lace can be.

Enjoy!
Karen Whooley

Learn to Delta Lace Crochet

DOUBLE CROCHET DELTA LACE

TREBLE CROCHET DELTA LACE

DOUBLE TREBLE CROCHET DELTA LACE

Creating Basic Delta Lace

The delta crochet mesh consists of triangles that alternate pointing up and down. In the diagrams, the upward triangles are made by skipping the indicated number of stitches, then working a double crochet, treble crochet or double treble crochet in the next stitch. Each of the following practice swatches contains the same number of delta stitches per row. As the stitches get taller, the spaces in the fabric increase.

DOUBLE CROCHET DELTA LACE
Double crochet delta lace stitch (dc delta lace st): (Dc, ch 3, dc) in indicated ch or st *(see illustration)*.

Beginning double crochet delta lace stitch (beg dc delta lace st): (Ch 6—*counts as first dc and ch-3*), dc) in indicated st *(see illustration)*.

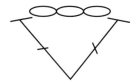

Double Crochet Delta Lace Stitch

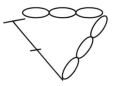

Beginning Double Crochet Delta Lace Stitch

Multiple of 4 + 7

Row 1: Ch 27, dc in 7th ch from hook *(beg 6 sk chs count as first dc and ch-3)*, *sk next 3 chs, **dc delta lace st** *(see above)* in next ch, rep from * across to last 4 chs, sk next 3 chs, dc in last ch, turn.

Row 2: Beg dc delta lace st *(see above)* in first dc, *sk next ch-3 sp, dc delta lace st in next dc, sk next dc, rep from * across to beg 6 sk chs, dc in 3rd ch of beg 6 sk chs, turn.

Row 3: Beg dc delta lace st in first dc, *sk next dc and ch-3 sp, dc delta lace st in next dc, rep from * across to beg ch-6, dc in 3rd ch of beg ch-6, turn.

Next rows: Rep row 3.

TREBLE CROCHET DELTA LACE

Treble crochet delta lace stitch (tr delta lace st):
(Tr, ch 4, tr) in indicated st *(see illustration).*

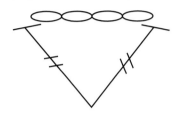

**Treble Crochet
Delta Lace Stitch**

Beginning treble crochet delta lace stitch (beg tr delta lace st): (Ch 8—*counts as first tr and ch-4,* tr) in indicated st *(see illustration).*

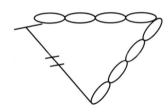

**Beginning Treble Crochet
Delta Lace Stitch**

Multiple of 5 + 9

Row 1: Ch 29, tr in 9th ch from hook, *sk next 4 chs, **tr delta lace st** *(see above)* in next ch, rep from * across to last 5 chs, sk next 4 chs, tr in last ch, turn.

Row 2: **Beg tr delta lace st** *(see above)* in first tr, *sk next ch-4 sp, tr delta lace st in next tr, sk next tr, rep from * across to beg sk 8 chs, tr in 4th ch of beg 8 sk chs, turn.

Row 3: Beg tr delta lace st in first tr, *sk next ch-4 sp, tr delta lace st in next tr, sk next tr, rep from * across to beg ch-8, tr in the 4th ch of beg ch-8, turn.

Next rows: Rep row 3.

DOUBLE TREBLE CROCHET DELTA LACE

Double treble crochet delta lace stitch (dtr delta lace st): (Dtr, ch 5, dtr) in indicated st *(see illustration).*

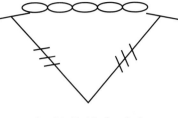

**Double Treble Crochet
Delta Lace Stitch**

Beginning double treble crochet delta lace stitch (beg dtr delta lace st): (Ch 10—*counts as first dtr and ch-5,* dtr) in indicated st *(see illustration).*

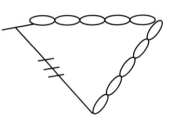

**Beginning Double Treble Crochet
Delta Lace Stitch**

Multiple of 6 + 11

Row 1: Ch 41, dtr in 11th ch from hook, *sk next 5 chs, **dtr delta lace st** *(see above)* in next ch, rep from * across to last 6 chs, sk next 5 chs, dtr in last ch, turn.

Row 2: **Beg dtr delta lace st** *(see above)* in first dtr, *sk next ch-5 sp, dtr delta lace st in next dtr, sk next dtr, rep from * across to beg sk 10 chs, dtr in 5th ch of beg 10 sk chs, turn.

Row 3: Beg dtr delta lace st in first dtr, *sk next ch-5 sp, dtr delta lace st in next dtr, sk next dtr, rep from * across to beg ch-10, dtr in 5th ch of beg ch-10, turn. ■

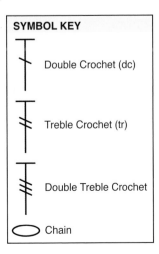

SYMBOL KEY

Double Crochet (dc)

Treble Crochet (tr)

Double Treble Crochet

Chain

Delta Lace Shawl

SKILL LEVEL

INTERMEDIATE

FINISHED SIZE

16 x 60 inches

MATERIALS

- Omega Sinfonia light (light worsted) weight yarn (3½ oz/232 yds/100g per skein):
  3 skeins #843 dark cinnamon
- Size E/4/3.5mm crochet hook or size needed to obtain gauge

GAUGE

3 tr delta lace sts = 3 inches; 6 tr delta lace st rows = 4 inches

PATTERN NOTE

Chain-8 at beginning of row counts as first treble crochet and chain-4 unless otherwise stated.

SPECIAL STITCHES

Treble crochet delta lace stitch (tr delta lace st): (Tr, ch 4, tr) in indicated st.

Beginning treble crochet delta lace stitch (beg tr delta lace st): (Ch 8—*see Pattern Notes*, tr) in indicated st.

INSTRUCTIONS
SHAWL
BODY

Row 1: Ch 89, tr in 9th ch from hook (*beg 8 sk chs and tr in 9th st count as beg tr delta lace st*), *sk next 4 chs, **tr delta lace st** (*see Special Stitches*) in next ch, rep from * across to last 5 chs, sk next 4 chs, tr in last ch, turn. (*16 tr delta lace sts*)

Row 2: Beg tr delta lace st (*see Special Stitches*) in first tr, *sk next ch-4 sp, tr delta lace st in next tr, rep from * across to beg 8 sk chs, tr in 4th ch of beg 8 sk chs, turn. (*16 tr delta lace sts*)

Row 3: Beg tr delta lace st in first tr, *sk next ch-4 sp, tr delta lace st in next tr, rep from * across to beg ch-8, tr in 4th ch of beg ch-8, turn. (*16 tr delta lace sts*)

Rep row 3 until Body is 56 inches long. **Do not fasten off.**

EDGING
FIRST END

Row 1 (RS): Ch 1, working in ch-4 sps and dc, evenly sp 98 sc across, turn.

Row 2: Working in **front lps** (*see Stitch Guide*), ch 1, sc in each st across, **turn**; now working in rem lps of row 1, sc in each st across, turn.

Row 3: Ch 1, sc in both lps of each of next 2 sts on rows 2 and 3, *sc in front lp of each of next 4 sts on row 2 only, **turn**, sc in back lp of row 3 and in rem lp of row 2 on each of next 4 sts, **turn**, sc in rem lp of each of next 4 sts on row 3, sc in both lps of each of next 2 sts on rows 2 and 3, rep from * across, turn.

Row 4: Ch 1, [sc in front lp of next sc, sc in **back lp** (*see Stitch Guide*) of next sc] across, turn.

Row 5: Ch 1, [sc in back lp of next sc, sc in front lp of next sc] across, turn.

Next rows: Rep rows 4 and 5 until Edging measures 2 inches wide. Fasten off.

2ND END

Row 1 (RS): Working in opposite side of beg ch, join in first st, ch 1, working in ch-4 sps and dc, evenly sp 98 sc across, turn.

Row 2: Working in front lps, ch 1, sc in each st across, **turn**; now working in rem lps of row 1, sc in each st across, turn.

Row 3: Ch 1, sc in both lps of each of next 2 sts on rows 2 and 3, *sc in front lp of each of next 4 sts on row 2 only, **turn**, sc in back lp of row 3 and in rem lp of row 2 on each of next 4 sts, **turn**, sc in rem lp of each of next 4 sts on row 3, sc in both lps of each of next 2 sts on rows 2 and 3, rep from * across, turn.

Row 4: Ch 1, [sc in front lp of next sc, sc in back lp of next sc] across, turn.

Row 5: Ch 1, [sc in back lp of next sc, sc in front lp of next sc] across, turn.

Next rows: Rep rows 4 and 5 until Edging measures 2 inches wide. Fasten off. ■

Delta Lace
Mobius Cowl

SKILL LEVEL

■■■▢
INTERMEDIATE

FINISHED SIZES

Instructions given fit 32–34-inch bust *(small)*; changes for 36–38-inch bust *(medium)*, 40–42-inch bust *(large)*, 44–46-inch bust *(X-large)*, 48–50-inch bust *(2X-large)* and 52–54-inch bust *(3X-large)* are in [ ].

FINISHED GARMENT MEASUREMENTS

Circumference: 36 [40, 44, 48, 52, 56] inches
Length (all sizes): 12 inches

MATERIALS

- Berroco Seduce Colors medium (worsted) weight yarn (1¼ oz/ 100 yds/40g per hank): 4 hanks #4494 chaos
- Size E/4/3.5mm crochet hook or size needed to obtain gauge

GAUGE

14 next foundation sc = 4 inches; 4 dc delta lace sts = 4½ inches; 8 dc delta lace st rows = 4 inches

PATTERN NOTES

Chain-6 at beginning of round counts as first double crochet and chain-3 unless otherwise stated.

Join rounds with slip stitch unless otherwise stated.

Do not turn at end of each round unless otherwise indicated.

When working round 2 on the mobius, you will be working on both sides of round 1, thus creating the fabric on both sides, working from the middle out. This is due to the 180-degree twist in the chain that creates the mobius shape.

Rounds 3–14 should begin and end with beginning chain right side up facing.

SPECIAL STITCHES

First foundation single crochet (first foundation sc): Ch 2, insert hook into 2nd ch from hook, yo, draw up lp, yo, draw through one lp on hook (*see A—ch-1 made*), yo, draw through 2 lps on hook (*see B and C—sc made*).

Next foundation single crochet (next foundation sc): *Insert hook in ch-1 made in first foundation sc (*see A*), yo, draw up lp, yo, pull through one lp on hook (*see B—ch-1 made*), yo, draw through 2 lps on hook (*see C and D—sc made*), rep from * as indicated.

Double crochet delta lace stitch (dc delta lace st): (Dc, ch 3, dc) in indicated st.

Beginning double crochet delta lace stitch (beg dc delta lace st): (Ch 6—*see Pattern Notes*, dc) in indicated st.

COWL

Rnd 1: With size E hook, **first foundation sc** (*see Special Stitches*), **next foundation sc** (*see Special Stitches*) 143 [149, 155, 161, 167, 173] times, twist beg of rnd 180 degrees, **join** (*see Pattern Notes*) in bottom of first foundation sc.

Rnd 2: Working in bottom of foundation sc, **beg dc delta lace st** (*see Special Stitches*) in same st as joining, *sk next 2 sts, **dc delta lace st** (*see Special Stitches*) in next st, rep from * around, join in 3rd ch of beg ch-6. (*96 [100, 104, 108, 112, 116] dc delta lace sts*)

Rnd 3: Beg dc delta lace st in same st as joining, *sk next ch-3 sp and dc, dc delta lace st in next dc, rep from * around, join in 3rd ch of beg ch-6.

Rnds 4–14: Rep rnd 3. Fasten off at end of last rnd. Weave in all ends. ∎

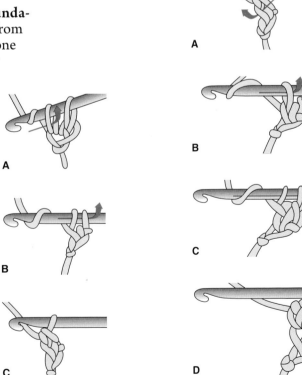

First Foundation Single Crochet   **Next Foundation Single Crochet**

Delta Lace Topper

SKILL LEVEL

INTERMEDIATE

FINISHED SIZE

One size fits most

FINISHED GARMENT MEASUREMENT

27 inches long from top of folded cuff to longest point

MATERIALS

- Omega Sinfonia light (light worsted) weight yarn (3½ oz/232 yds/100g per skein):
    4 skeins #816 teal
- Sizes E/4/3.5mm and F/5/3.75mm crochet hooks or size needed to obtain gauge

GAUGE

Size F hook: 3 tr delta lace sts = 3½ inches; 5 tr delta lace st rows = 4 inches

PATTERN NOTES

Chain-9 at beginning of row or round counts as first treble crochet and chain-4 unless otherwise stated.

Join rounds with slip stitch unless otherwise stated.

Do not turn at end of each round unless otherwise indicated.

Increases at either side of topper are to be worn at left and right sides so points are longer at wrists.

SPECIAL STITCHES

First foundation single crochet (first foundation sc): Ch 2, insert hook into 2nd ch from hook, yo, draw up lp, yo, draw through one lp on hook (*see A—ch-1 made*), yo, draw through 2 lps on hook (*see B and C—sc made*).

Next foundation single crochet (next foundation sc): *Insert hook in ch-1 made in first foundation sc (*see A*), yo, draw up lp, yo, pull through one lp on hook (*see B—ch-1 made*), yo, draw through 2 lps on hook (*see C and D—sc made*), rep from * as indicated.

Treble crochet delta lace stitch (tr delta lace st): (Tr, ch 4, tr) in indicated st.

Beginning treble crochet delta lace stitch (beg tr delta lace st): (Ch 9—*see Pattern Notes*, tr) in indicated st.

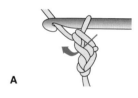

A

B

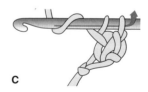

C

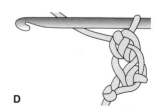

D

A

B

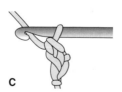

C

First Foundation Single Crochet

Next Foundation Single Crochet

Treble crochet delta lace increase (tr delta lace inc): Tr delta lace st twice in indicated st.

INSTRUCTIONS
SHAWL
BODY

Rnd 1: With size F hook, **first foundation sc** (*see Special Stitches*), **next foundation sc** (*see Special Stitches*) 103 times, **join** (*see Pattern Notes*) in first foundation sc.

Rnd 2: **Beg tr delta lace st** (*see Special Stitches*) in same st as joining, *sk next 3 sts**, **tr delta lace st** (*see Special Stitches*) in next st, rep from * around, ending last rep at **, join in 5th ch of beg ch-9. (*26 tr delta lace sts*)

Rnd 3: Beg tr delta lace st in same st as joining, *[sk next ch-4 sp and next tr, tr delta lace st in next tr] 11 times, sk next ch-4 sp and tr, **tr delta lace inc** (*see Special Stitches*) in next tr**, rep from * once, ending last rep at **, join in 5th ch of beg ch-9. (*28 tr delta lace sts*)

Rnd 4: Beg tr delta lace st in same st as joining, *[sk next ch-4 sp and tr, tr delta lace st in next tr] around to next tr delta lace inc, sk next ch-4 sp and tr, tr delta lace inc in next tr, rep from * around, join in 5th ch of beg ch-9 (*30 tr delta lace sts*)

Rnds 5–25: Rep rnd 4. (*70 tr delta lace sts at end of last rnd*)

Rnd 26: Ch 1, sc in same st as joining, (dc, {ch 1, dc} 6 times) in next ch-4 sp**, sk next tr, sc in next tr, rep from * around, ending last rep at **, join in first sc. Fasten off.

COLLAR

Row 1: With size E hook, join in opposite side of foundation sc at center back of Body, ch 31, sc in **back bar** (*see illustration*) of 2nd ch from hook and in each rem ch across, sl st in each of next 2 foundation sc on Body, turn. (*30 sc, 2 sl sts*)

Back Bar of Chain

Row 2: Sk next 2 sl sts, sc in **back lp** (*see Stitch Guide*) of each sc across, turn. (*30 sc*)

Row 3: Ch 1, sc in back lp of each sc across, sl st in each of next 2 foundation sc on Body, turn. (*30 sc, 2 sl sts*)

Rows 4–104: [Rep rows 2 and 3 alternately] 51 times, ending last rep with row 2. Leaving 18-inch tail, fasten off at end of last row.

ASSEMBLY

With WS facing, using 18-inch tail, sew rows 1 and 104 tog. Fasten off and weave in ends. ■

Delta Lace
Skull Cap
& Scarf

SKILL LEVEL

EASY

FINISHED MEASUREMENT
20 inches in circumference

MATERIALS
- Plymouth Yarns Fantasy Naturale medium (worsted) weight yarn (3½ oz/140 yds/100g per skein): 1 skein #9966 camouflage
- Size I/9/5.5mm crochet hook or size needed to obtain gauge

GAUGE
Rnds 1–3 = 4 inches in diameter

PATTERN NOTES
Chain-3 at beginning of round counts as first double crochet unless otherwise stated.

Chain-6 at beginning of round counts as first double crochet and chain-3 unless otherwise stated.

Join rounds with slip stitch unless otherwise stated.

SPECIAL STITCHES
Double crochet delta lace stitch (dc delta lace st): (Dc, ch 3, dc) in indicated st.

Beginning double crochet delta lace stitch (beg dc delta lace st): (Ch 6—*see Pattern Notes*, dc) in indicated st.

INSTRUCTIONS
CAP
Rnd 1: Ch 4, 11 dc in 4th ch from hook (*3 sk chs count as first dc*), **join** (*see Pattern Notes*) in 3rd ch of beg 3 sk chs. (*12 dc*)

Rnd 2: Ch 3 (*see Pattern Notes*), dc in same st as beg ch-3, 2 dc in each dc around, join in top of beg ch-3. (*24 dc*)

Rnd 3: Ch 3, 2 dc in next dc, [dc in next dc, 2 dc in next dc] around, join in top of beg ch-3. (*36 dc*)

Rnd 4: Ch 3, dc in same st as beg ch-3, dc in each of next 2 dc, [2 dc in next dc, dc in each of next 2 dc] around, join in top of beg ch-3. (*48 dc*)

Rnd 5: Ch 3, dc in each of next 2 dc, 2 dc in next dc, [dc in each of next 3 dc, 2 dc in next dc] around, join in top of beg ch-3. (*60 dc*)

Rnd 6: **Beg dc delta lace st** (*see Special Stitches*) in top of beg ch-3, *sk next 3 dc, **dc delta lace st** (*see Special Stitches*) in next dc, rep from * around to last 3 dc, sk last 3 dc, join in 3rd ch of beg ch-6. (*15 dc delta lace sts*)

Rnd 7: Beg dc delta lace st in top of beg ch-3, *sk next ch-3 sp**, dc delta lace st in next dc, sk next dc, rep from * around, ending last rep at **, join in 3rd ch of beg ch-6.

Rnds 8–10: Rep rnd 7.

Rnd 11: Ch 3, dc in each dc and 2 dc in each ch-3 sp around, join in top of beg ch-3. (*60 dc*)

Rnd 12: Ch 1, **reverse sc** (*see Stitch Guide*) in each dc around, join in first st. Fasten off. Weave in all ends.

SCARF
SKILL LEVEL

EASY

FINISHED MEASUREMENT
5 x 64 inches

MATERIALS
- Plymouth Yarn Fantasy Naturale medium (worsted) weight yarn (3½ oz/140 yds/100g per skein): 2 skeins #9966 camouflage
- Size I/9/5.5mm crochet hook or size needed to obtain gauge

GAUGE
3 dc delta lace sts = 4 inches; 4 dc delta lace st rows = 4 inches

PATTERN NOTE

Chain-6 at beginning of row counts as first double crochet and chain-3 unless otherwise stated.

SPECIAL STITCHES

Double crochet delta lace stitch (dc delta lace st): (Dc, ch 3, dc) in indicated st.

Beginning double crochet delta lace st (beg dc delta lace st): (**Ch 6**—*see Pattern Note*, dc) in indicated st.

INSTRUCTIONS
SCARF

Row 1: Ch 23, dc in 7th ch from hook *(beg 6 sk chs and first dc count as first dc delta lace st)*, *sk next 3 chs, **dc delta lace st** *(see Special Stitches)* in next ch, rep from * twice, sk next 3 chs, dc in last ch, turn. *(4 dc delta lace sts)*

Row 2: Beg dc delta lace st *(see Special Stitches)* in first dc, *sk next dc and ch-3 sp, dc delta lace st in next dc, rep from * twice, dc in 3rd ch of beg 6 sk chs, turn.

Row 3: Beg dc delta lace st in first dc, *sk next dc and next ch-3 sp, dc delta lace st in next dc, rep from * twice, sk next dc, dc in 3rd ch of beg ch-6, turn.

Next rows: Rep row 3 until Scarf measures 60 inches or desired length. Fasten off at end of last row. Weave in ends. ■

STITCH GUIDE

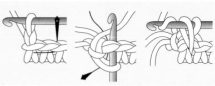

STITCH ABBREVIATIONS

beg	begin/begins/beginning
bpdc	back post double crochet
bpsc	back post single crochet
bptr	back post treble crochet
CC	contrasting color
ch(s)	chain(s)
ch-	refers to chain or space previously made (i.e., ch-1 space)
ch sp(s)	chain space(s)
cl(s)	cluster(s)
cm	centimeter(s)
dc	double crochet (singular/plural)
dc dec	double crochet 2 or more stitches together, as indicated
dec	decrease/decreases/decreasing
dtr	double treble crochet
ext	extended
fpdc	front post double crochet
fpsc	front post single crochet
fptr	front post treble crochet
g	gram(s)
hdc	half double crochet
hdc dec	half double crochet 2 or more stitches together, as indicated
inc	increase/increases/increasing
lp(s)	loop(s)
MC	main color
mm	millimeter(s)
oz	ounce(s)
pc	popcorn(s)
rem	remain/remains/remaining
rep(s)	repeat(s)
rnd(s)	round(s)
RS	right side
sc	single crochet (singular/plural)
sc dec	single crochet 2 or more stitches together, as indicated
sk	skip/skipped/skipping
sl st(s)	slip stitch(es)
sp(s)	space(s)/spaced
st(s)	stitch(es)
tog	together
tr	treble crochet
trtr	triple treble
WS	wrong side
yd(s)	yard(s)
yo	yarn over

YARN CONVERSION

OUNCES TO GRAMS		GRAMS TO OUNCES	
1	28.4	25	⅞
2	56.7	40	1⅔
3	85.0	50	1¾
4	113.4	100	3½

UNITED STATES		UNITED KINGDOM
sl st (slip stitch)	=	sc (single crochet)
sc (single crochet)	=	dc (double crochet)
hdc (half double crochet)	=	htr (half treble crochet)
dc (double crochet)	=	tr (treble crochet)
tr (treble crochet)	=	dtr (double treble crochet)
dtr (double treble crochet)	=	ttr (triple treble crochet)
skip	=	miss

Single crochet decrease (sc dec): (Insert hook, yo, draw lp through) in each of the sts indicated, yo, draw through all lps on hook.

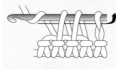

Example of 2-sc dec

Half double crochet decrease (hdc dec): (Yo, insert hook, yo, draw lp through) in each of the sts indicated, yo, draw through all lps on hook.

Example of 2-hdc dec

Reverse Single Crochet (reverse sc): Ch 1. Skip first st. [Working from left to right, insert hook in next st from front to back, draw up lp on hook, yo, and draw through both lps on hook.]

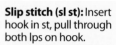

Chain (ch): Yo, pull through lp on hook.

Single crochet (sc): Insert hook in st, yo, pull through st, yo, pull through both lps on hook.

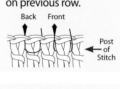

Double crochet (dc): Yo, insert hook in st, yo, pull through st, [yo, pull through 2 lps] twice.

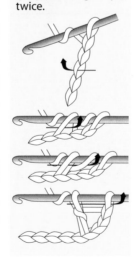

Double crochet decrease (dc dec): (Yo, insert hook, yo, draw loop through, draw through 2 lps on hook) in each of the sts indicated, yo, draw through all lps on hook.

Example of 2-dc dec

Front loop (front lp) Back loop (back lp)

Front Loop   Back Loop

Front post stitch (fp): Back post stitch (bp): When working post st, insert hook from right to left around post st on previous row.

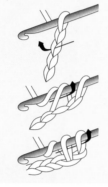

Back   Front

Post of Stitch

Half double crochet (hdc): Yo, insert hook in st, yo, pull through st, yo, pull through all 3 lps on hook.

Double treble crochet (dtr): Yo 3 times, insert hook in st, yo, pull through st, [yo, pull through 2 lps] 4 times.

Treble crochet decrease (tr dec): Holding back last lp of each st, tr in each of the sts indicated, yo, pull through all lps on hook.

Example of 2-tr dec

Slip stitch (sl st): Insert hook in st, pull through both lps on hook.

Chain Color Change (ch color change) Yo with new color, draw through last lp on hook.

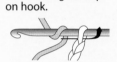

Double Crochet Color Change (dc color change) Drop first color, yo with new color, draw through last 2 lps of st.

Treble crochet (tr): Yo twice, insert hook in st, yo, pull through st, [yo, pull through 2 lps] 3 times.

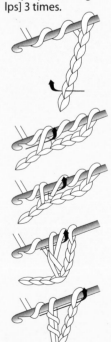

Metric
Conversion
Charts

METRIC CONVERSIONS

yards	x	.9144	=	metres (m)
yards	x	91.44	=	centimetres (cm)
inches	x	2.54	=	centimetres (cm)
inches	x	25.40	=	millimetres (mm)
inches	x	.0254	=	metres (m)

centimetres	x	.3937	=	inches
metres	x	1.0936	=	yards

INCHES INTO MILLIMETRES & CENTIMETRES (Rounded off slightly)

inches	mm	cm	inches	cm	inches	cm	inches	cm
1/8	3	0.3	5	12.5	21	53.5	38	96.5
1/4	6	0.6	5 1/2	14	22	56	39	99
3/8	10	1	6	15	23	58.5	40	101.5
1/2	13	1.3	7	18	24	61	41	104
5/8	15	1.5	8	20.5	25	63.5	42	106.5
3/4	20	2	9	23	26	66	43	109
7/8	22	2.2	10	25.5	27	68.5	44	112
1	25	2.5	11	28	28	71	45	114.5
1 1/4	32	3.2	12	30.5	29	73.5	46	117
1 1/2	38	3.8	13	33	30	76	47	119.5
1 3/4	45	4.5	14	35.5	31	79	48	122
2	50	5	15	38	32	81.5	49	124.5
2 1/2	65	6.5	16	40.5	33	84	50	127
3	75	7.5	17	43	34	86.5		
3 1/2	90	9	18	46	35	89		
4	100	10	19	48.5	36	91.5		
4 1/2	115	11.5	20	51	37	94		

KNITTING NEEDLES CONVERSION CHART

Canada/U.S.	0	1	2	3	4	5	6	7	8	9	10	10½	11	13	15
Metric (mm)	2	2¼	2¾	3¼	3½	3¾	4	4½	5	5½	6	6½	·8	9	10

CROCHET HOOKS CONVERSION CHART

Canada/U.S.	1/B	2/C	3/D	4/E	5/F	6/G	8/H	9/I	10/J	10½/K	N
Metric (mm)	2.25	2.75	3.25	3.5	3.75	4.25	5	5.5	6	6.5	9.0

RETAIL STORES: If you would like to carry this pattern book or any other DRG publications, visit DRGwholesale.com

Every effort has been made to ensure that the instructions in this publication are complete and accurate. We cannot, however, take responsibility for human error, typographical mistakes or variations in individual work. Please visit AnniesCustomerCare.com to check for pattern updates.

ISBN: 978-1-59635-366-4

1 2 3 4 5 6 7 8 9